Sea Grapes and Sea Oats

Sea Grapes and Sea Oats

Jeffrey Jay Niehaus

RESOURCE *Publications* · Eugene, Oregon

SEA GRAPES AND SEA OATS

Resource Publications
An Imprint of Wipf and Stock Publishers
199 W. 8th Ave., Suite 3
Eugene, OR 97401

www.wipfandstock.com

PAPERBACK ISBN: 978-1-5326-5659-0
HARDCOVER ISBN: 978-1-5326-5660-6
EBOOK ISBN: 978-1-5326-5661-3

Manufactured in the U.S.A.

FOR

ERIN & ANNIKA

beauty is truth, truth beauty

CONTENTS

AFTER SONNETS | 1

POEM TO ROTTING APPLES | 2

BIRD OF PARADISE | 3

COFFEA | 4

TWO PALMS | 5

SALISBURY CATHEDRAL | 6

CASTILLO DE SAN MARCOS | 7

HALLS OF MONTEZUMA | 8

PALM BEACH INLET | 9

DANZAS FANTASTICAS | 10

PADDLES AND PALMS | 11

DIE TOTENINSEL | 12

DAS GROßE WERK | 13

PUG BARK ON | 14

LUMINOUS MOMENT | 15

FLAGLER MANSION | 16

SHARK THOUGHTS | 17

BOSTON BAY | 18

HÄNDEL AND COMPANY | 19

FISHING BOATS | 20

AQUATICA | 21

TV | 22

JAMAICA COTTAGE | 23

FOGGY MORNING | 24

AQUATIC WONDER | 25

EVERGLADES NATIONAL PARK | 26

WRECKERS OFF THE COAST OF NORTHUMBRIA | 27

SNAPPER | 28

ANDROMEDA | 29

A CALL | 30

20,000 LEAGUES UNDER THE SEA | 31

A SKUNK | 32

CONTENTS

SOLAR DAY | 33

POET AND POEM | 34

COCKER SPANIEL PUP | 35

ONE DAY A POSTMAN | 36

ELGAR HOUSE | 37

A PATIO AND PALMS | 38

DEL MAR | 39

CARMEL ET SUA | 40

STRAWBERRY HARVEST | 41

WHAT WOULD YOU DO? | 42

SUMMER STORM | 43

SEA PUG | 44

MUNICH QUARTET | 45

CHAUSSER MAUDIT | 46

A PAUSE AT GARMISCH | 47

PROLIFIC | 48

COCONUT BOYS | 49

ANTIQUING | 50

STONE AND THOMAS | 51

AMBERJACK | 52

EIN POKAL | 53

PORTLAND CAFÉ | 54

PORTLAND CAFÉ REDUX | 55

UNCA $CROOGE'S MONEY BIN | 56

EXSPECTANS | 57

A SUNSET | 58

INTERLOPER | 59

YOUR FOURTH | 60

BEETHOVEN'S BIRTHDAY | 61

ART ἐπ' ἐσχάτου τῶν ἡμερῶν τούτων | 62

LAKE WORTH AFTER LATIN CLASS | 63

SOUTHERN COMFORT | 64

YOU WAIT | 65

WRIT IN WATER | 66

CONTENTS

SEA GRAPE WINE | 67

PALM BEACH INTRACOASTAL | 68

FRAGMENTS | 69

PENELOPE BARKER HOUSE | 70

MUSIC | 71

BOAT IN THE SAND | 72

PATIO AT NORTH PALM BEACH | 73

CUMQUAT BASKET | 74

PORTALS | 75

SUMMER STORM | 76

SHALLOW SOUL | 77

O VOLUMES | 78

OUR SHATTERED AGE | 79

CATHEDRAL OR NAUTILUS | 80

EN FUEGO | 81

ADMIRATION | 82

A CUP | 83

BEAUTIFUL THINGS | 84

FISH STORIES | 85

FREEDOM | 86

PREPARATORY | 87

NEMO'S FARE | 88

CONCH MORNING | 89

PELICAN | 90

SMALL COWRIES | 91

A NEW DAY | 92

WEARY | 93

ONCE PARADISE | 94

ORCHESTRAL COLOR | 95

MOON AND WAVES | 96

HEINRICH'S | 97

SEA GRAPE | 98

SEA OAT | 99

ISLAND SHEAF | 100

AFTER SONNETS

After sonnets how about a siesta
Sombrero in hot sun over your face
No sound around, but tumbleweed
Casually rolling past could be
A low, silent breeze after them—

As you repose against an old fence?

On a southwestern afternoon
You could dream of chilis, enchiladas
Jalapeños and Scoville units
And not have to worry about tomorrow
Because endorphins took it all away
Before it could bother you today.

As you relax upon some old wood
Gastronomics offer short delay.

POEM TO ROTTING APPLES

Why would you compose a poem to rotting apples?
—MAGGI

Why would one compose a poem, you ask,
To rotting apples?

            Although long ago
As humans ordinarily count long
Schiller loved to do so—and who knows
Who brought the apples to his study
Or what inspiration entered him
When nostrils dilated to catch and hold
For elevated moments those aromas
Just a rotten apple could produce?

So now you have conjured a new poem,
A sonnet I would hardly have composed,
Only, I spoke of Schiller—and you mocked.

So mockery and playfulness gave birth
To what a rotten apple has brought forth.

BIRD OF PARADISE

Paradisaeidae (your Latin name)
Accustomed to New Guinea and her islands
But also now and then in Florida
One could spot in yard or garden
Your tropical outrageous orange crest—
A crown of many colors honestly
And not one color of a Florida fruit.

I saw you only rarely as a boy
In our subtropical peninsula.

West Palm Beach was almost part of sand
And sea and plants and animals could be
Sublimely indifferent to us.

Who could own such a crown and be
So tranquil beyond words

O *rara avis*

COFFEA

Coffea I love you—imagine
How you can stimulate
Any hour I hope to enjoy you—

O save a soul from Yankee lethargy

Coffea Arabica whose glossy leaves
Although lovely hardly offer us
A clue as to what pink or purple berries
Can do for a desperate soul.

So transport me to India, Cameroon
Or anywhere in South America
Or even better take me to Jamaica
And her Blue Mountains

                          or rather her coast

And Sugar Mill Restaurant

                                where I can sip

Coffea

        by an abandoned water wheel

TWO PALMS

Two palm trees at North Palm Beach
So long ago when Florida
Was simple—undeveloped as men say

You saw them arcing tall and narrow and
You thought they should be on a post card
Or rather, thought they were

                                so unreal

Those palms looked to one from England.

I could reassure you they were not
Imaginary or some sort of art
Posing as palms

                  on a public shore.

SALISBURY CATHEDRAL

Astounding mass of stonework on grass,
Flat and rolled as one may often see
In England's green and pleasant

                                          land

Masonry to Our Lady a spire,
Tallest in the isle—no aspiration
Beyond a hope of heaven.

                                 May no hubris

Undo our offering.

                              Once, a skeptic,
I ambled on your plain and saw
Your solemn cloister and the eloquent
Chaste fan vault of your chapter house

And hardly understood how such work
Could honor God who was supernal

Only older would I know
Architecture

                    can become a song.

CASTILLO DE SAN MARCOS

Old castle at Matanzas Bay you guard
Only your memories.

                    Your sturdy walls
Fashioned of coquina stone and proof
Against the rude assault of any foe—
Your stone absorbed a cannon ball at impact
And put a halt to its career.

                    Banners
Of four empires have floated over you
Imperial Spain, Great Britain and the short
Confederacy and today our own
Or should I say imperium of our States
Who love imperial fruit but not repute

How far apart from them

                    to stand

A tourist on a rampart of coquina
And look across a bay of Florida.

HALLS OF MONTEZUMA

Montezuma II how could you know
Rampant lust beyond even your wont
For gold?

              How noble your broad avenue
How novel in your capital a cage
Of many birds chosen from a world
And canals of fluent imperial trade
O teocali towering above—
Home of a Sun you all adored—
Till Quetzalcoatl came to you one day
Cortez to us and brought you down

Your blood soaked altar vacant now

                      and now

Your history alluded to in song

Beyond that

          who recalls your golden calendar

Your chocolatl or your pinioned cape?

PALM BEACH INLET

A solar afternoon and sand so hot
Soles would burn as you ran across it
O glory of young days

                    Parked illegally

Along an alleyway at a hotel
On the waterfront so I could lug
A *Dacor* scuba tank a short way
And stand before your shallows, your pump house
And rusty crane so picturesque
And admire girls whose bronzed skin
Sang of Florida and don my tank.

Sun and sand and sea all spoke of you
And won my soul to love

                    and as I sank

Among the warm, shallow waters I

Could hardly imagine any other.

DANZAS FANTASTICAS

Turina, music full of the warm south
For any European and for me
A warm escape into some paradise—

Not Paradise nor only memory
Of North Palm Beach and coconut palm trees
But somehow just partway—

                                my own idea

Almost divine, or half divine maybe—
A personal savor of Paradise.

A man could fancy he was almost God
But I would rather want a palm beach
I know I cannot have,

                        for such a moment

Approaches Paradise.

PADDLES AND PALMS

Some years ago I sat and wrote about
A former life in Palm Springs, Atlanta,
New Haven and

                  once more Florida

Almost as a random ping pong ball
Or metal ball in a penny arcade
Rolls or bounces around unaware
Of a paddle (or what one can do)

Or what a future course could be—

                        I also

Caromed from one state to another.

So others also in a random land—
No matter with or without palms—may do,
Do do, and hopeless as I was.

                    So now

What comfort can I offer them

                  but you?

DIE TOTENINSEL

A glassy lake—slate colored
And green from shade of cypress trees—
Architecture, as of Roman caverns
Rectangular with architrave expectant
That flank the tall gaunt cypress,
Gray sky beyond untouchable and now
A skiff approaches, at the oars a woman
A Nordic type and at the prow what looks
A table set as for communion
White tablecloth and a tall white cowled figure
Before the cloth. An old proverb
Denn die Toten reiten schnell sounds false—
On that island and as one approaches
No pulse, no hurry prods.

DAS GROßE WERK

Callimachus once wrote a big book
Was a big bad or words so translated—
μέγα βιβλίον μέγα κακόν—
Almost

       a Hebrew parallelism

Thomas Mann wrote about a master
Who suffered and was great—Richard Wagner—
Romantic hunger for grandeur
And large works

          Nonetheless

Today's critic may find
The fault is in our dull quotidian

                       not

In an old aesthetic.

PUG BARK ON

O pug bark on at any passer by
You and you alone can understand
What zeal to defend our home
What noble undertaking as a guardian
Or what animal spirits drove you
To such a torrent of admonition—
A throaty declaration of your stand
Or patent xenophobia.

                What matter?
I love you nonetheless—may love you more
Because you say our turf is your own turf
Our small studious world your own world
And in your unambiguous alliance
To both master and mistress do declare
A global insularity.

LUMINOUS MOMENT

Boynton Inlet on an afternoon
In 1957 as power boats
Took folks deep sea fishing

      and a shack

Wore palm fronds

     fringe almost like thatch

Sold captain's hats for boys

      and parents looked

For another charter boat.

     Under the sun

Along the inlet wall many stood
And hoped to catch a fish in water lucid
And turquoise blue under a cloudless sky
And one could see a shark meander by
Only concerned with his own business—
Unaware of spectators above

Innocent of

    his watery thought

FLAGLER MANSION

Flagler Mansion on a sultry day

A Roman portico before a doorway
A hall, armchairs as large as any throne
A lofty ceiling and large cameos
Almost as though a Michelangelo
Offered art a baron could afford

And on the back lawn a railroad car
Polished wood, leather and brass appointments
Spoke of moneyed comfort in its day
Close by our Intracoastal Waterway.

SHARK THOUGHTS

Palm Beach Inlet

                and the ocean

Stalled at neap tide and I hung still
Supported just by scuba gear

                   above

A small cave formed by fallen rocks

And in the cave a lazy shark

Sun and shadow on his dappled back

Also hung and looked at me askance
As if I were a random morsel
Not easy to digest

              not worth the trouble.

BOSTON BAY

One sunny afternoon at home

                                          wander far away

Boston Bay a tropical escape
Coals of allspice wood gray

                             hot

Local black men
Patois not accessible to me

Jerk pork

                   taste buds astounded

A memory forever

Returns and goes away
As soon as it came

HÄNDEL AND COMPANY

A Händel keyboard suite

         on radio

A sunny afternoon and our pug
Small sprawl on a sofa
And now Brahms' Fourth.

         A wondrous age

Bruno Walter wrote
Any who wanted music
At home had to play—there was no radio

No dial to turn

         no button to depress

So product of a tired age I sit
Brahms in the background
Last of the great classical Caesars
One scholar dubbed him

FISHING BOATS

Colorful boats four in a row

                       and four

Not far offshore

                two almost grounded

But four onshore on sand
Red blue green blue and no fish
Or fishermen around

                  van Gogh

How warm or cool was it that June day
Under blue sky

              whose clouds almost alive

Do they show you were half mad?

Happy madness understands
Sand, boats, clouds, waves

                 and oil

AQUATICA

Waves wavelets and ripples
Water shallow and lucid so
I saw grains of sand beige minute
Shell fragments too of larger homes
Abandoned by their occupants,
Subdivided by the random sea

Ocean you pacify and comfort
In memoria

        so long ago

I knew your aquatic wonder
A sophomore Latin student—

        Mare nostrum—

Shards of an old life rounded now
Softened by the work of many waters

You love me—a warm memory
On a brisk April day

        close to winter

Remote from you

        dea

TV

A cornucopia a boy could
Own when Maverick was a brand new show
And Fred worked at a gravel pit and Barney
Was gullible and good.

How many Fridays

Rodney and I watched

We had pizza

From Papaleo's shop not far away—

—a farmer's market outside West Palm Beach

So many Fridays I cannot recount

Only

Our evenings were innocent

Compared

JAMAICA COTTAGE

A cottage on a small campus
A breeze may come and ruffle your curtains
A tropic song

              80° plus in January

Sunning at ten o'clock and glad
No duty called beyond

                  a sun tan

Aloft on a telephone cable
An air plant commands wonder

Epiphyte of impulsive bloom
Purple orange and full of *tropicalia*

And at night just before
False dawn

           a howl of many hounds

Uncanny ululation

Made me wonder

                what unruly ghosts

Abandoned sunken ships

FOGGY MORNING

Morning fog

        oak and maple branches

Grope not

        moribund they look

March in Massachusetts

Naked branches of life

AQUATIC WONDER

Aquatic wonder I would long
A young lad for your warm shallows

Don a mask and snorkel and swim out
In deeper water

                       and more full of awe

See those undulations

                    sandy

Sea bottom below

Only a fathom—enough to start
Short intakes, palpitations—

No shell on those untrodden waves
No call to explore

                   only

EVERGLADES NATIONAL PARK

A boy I saw you also a man
Airboats astounded me
How one skipped over water and saw grass
At ease in a swamp at home in you

As a man a young man also
I rode in one astonished

                    a tourist

By what someone had made, astounded
At alligators grown ugly
Old and fat but still able to run—
Outrun one of us

                    Florida!

Home of alligator boar and heron
Coconut cumquat all flora
And fauna who know

                    hours

Of tooth and claw

                    under the sun

26

WRECKERS OFF THE COAST
OF NORTHUMBRIA

Twelve foot or more those waves

                                  going to pound

A northern shore and local folk also
Who struggle about some thing

                              not so obvious

As Turner loved to paint objects

                            dissolved

More color than clarity—more luminous
Than substantial—and yet he was
Composer of light and sound—sound visible
In waves that pound

                      and storm that lashes them

And far away clouds tower dark
A show of sunshine more remote
A shadow castle hovers

What masted ship offshore

                          a steamboat chugs

SNAPPER

Uncle Victor after he caught
A snapping turtle one foot long
Or so

       I was a boy and he was big

Came to Granddad's basement

I looked on

          Dad told me
A snapper could be dangerous

          as uncle Victor
Grabbed a broom and held
A hatchet and would draw
Old turtle by the broom
Who showed his large muscular neck
And lost his head.

          Not many hours ago
At Brushy Fork in murky water he
Swam among dead branches

             hungry

ANDROMEDA

Andromeda bound to a rock because
Your mother boasted, and bound to become
Woman to a dragon or sea monster
Somewhere on a southern coast

                         a place

Geographers cannot locate

A boy in a far different south
Homer unknown to me Ovid also
Unknown but with a 2.4" refractor
I looked for you as autumn came

                        and brought

Football close to Lake Worth Junior High
School, studious hours

                   some moonless nights

At last a galaxy that bore your name
A boy astronomer

            found

A CALL

Too soon another call
To other work

           to pages, books

I never wrote and ought to write
For old academia—or no
Compose long pages of comfortable prose
Not common in our guild maybe and yet
A relic of some hallowed bygone age
Or something like

                you know me well enough

And know where I would be

                    an I could

A sandpiper scampers up and down
As waves flow in and out and small holes
Show up in wet sand and sand fleas
Burrow a small wash zone

                 full of hope

For food

            and are food

20,000 LEAGUES UNDER THE SEA

Walt Disney made a movie and a cast
Of notables played such actors
As compose mythic lore

                        Captain Nemo—

Whose name was no one—anonymous Destroyer
Of all who made war

                also made war

On warships—a modern irony

Came forth

           from the head of Zeus such wisdom?

A SKUNK

Our black cocker spaniel
"Rocket"

        because I was a boy and loved space

We drove
West of Martins Ferry
Dad bought an acre undulant
And apple trees

We harvested

        Curious Rocket

A stranger encounter

Skunk oil

        Mother soaped him

Natheless

SOLAR DAY

O solar appetite

          you may arouse

Slowly imagination—
An image or two—
So one who suns in summer may absorb
Inspiration almost tropical

And afterward compose

                or fancy

One sat by a banyan and lofty palms
Rustled above from a breeze off the 'Glades

Until

POET AND POEM

A poet ought to be
Good

      a truism you say? But no

Books of poetry modern postmodern
Show how far away

            O good Spirit

Forgive them for

               fragmented as I was

So many wrote and did not know
A poet who made all

And is good

COCKER SPANIEL PUP

Dad took me to a farm
In our Ohio hills

          and there I saw

A black cocker spaniel pup
On a floor in an open box
Full of his small brothers

Pups not long ago blind

A day later Dad could collect him
And in my bedroom on North Seventh Street
A small cardboard box in a corner
Was his bed

        and I was home

ONE DAY A POSTMAN

Mom was a secretary
At Tri–State Asphalt
Dad was on the road
Selling paint to farmers
I was at school

— a neighbor told my folks
A postman came with a big stick
And Rocket would bark
Chained to a doghouse

in carcere et vinclis

The postman almost like a ruffian guard
Unauthorized by those who owned the house
Came down hard

Always after that

Rocket hated

      men

        in uniform

ELGAR HOUSE

Banks of colorful flowers in May
Arranged and not—an English garden—

A cottage of umber brick
Two storeys—a museum now—

Upstairs especially
Memorabilia for us

Small slippers worn on the day
Edward VII dubbed him Sir

A signed photograph of Richard Strauss
Who called him Meister and master of colour

And T. E. Lawrence comes to mind
Who got a record of the Second Symphony
From a local library
And listened
And wrote to Elgar
And said

        "One seems to stop there."

A PATIO AND PALMS

Spring afternoon—San Diego
On a patio of a house
Crowned with Spanish tiles

                        stucco walls

And I oblivious a moment
Under blue sky and warm sun

Comforted by sun, breeze, rustle of palms

Not in Florida

                our other coast

Almost vacuous

DEL MAR

Coast of rumpled sandy cliffs and paths
Across grassy slopes above the sea

Wooden benches overlook

Girls in bikinis scraggly older men
Who mar the scene or add color
Families variegated, at play

And twisted trees accustomed to the wind
Offshore, constant

                              and

Canary Island date palms

At roadside some eucalyptus
Small palmettos

Shops above commuter rail upscale
Pubs and restaurants

CARMEL ET SUA

A uniformity of stucco houses
Spanish tile roofs ochre some faded

Palms and palmettos many succulents
Small patches of grass now and then

An occasional lizard who may nap
Undisturbed in afternoon sun

An Acura or Lexus passes by
Does not disturb our equilibrium

Various and uniform
Affluent houses *sans* character

Should you abandon wood structures
Or old brick houses in New England

For expansive palms and lizards

And such

STRAWBERRY HARVEST

A family morning hard by Palomar
Hispanic girl in shorts at the counter
Amiable almost flirtatious
Also beautiful

now strawberries

Long elevated rows
Black plastic mulch
Watered from below red luscious fruit
Some round and available
Some ripening or in the bud

Dirt on our sandals after
One cost of the harvest

you declare

So say I and so agreement comes
Comfortably on a sunny morning
In southern California

WHAT WOULD YOU DO?

What would you do

                    you would devour me

I know full well you would pounce like a lion
Fangs always red from a last victim

Our passing slower than decay
Although decay can seem a living death

But till the scythe

                 you do crouch at the door

A door not of wood stone or metal

And wanting invitation

                 do test my mettle

SUMMER STORM

Dark as old lead at your base
Cumulus thundercloud far away
Powered upward by hot air, soon
Upon us

        Baal or Enlil also

Untrue god in thunderclap
Come to water our fecund land

Archaic notion handed down
From two who saw You

                in angry mode

As a boy in Florida I saw you
And only loved the drama of your coming

A hero nebulous mutates his form
Draws wind across the sea from shore

Grows powerful from all contributions

As a god may from

           adorers

SEA PUG

Our pug although he saw not
Pacific in a placid mood Atlantic
In a stormy mood or Caribbean
In any mood at all

And so was no sea dog

                        Still

You dubbed him a sea pug

He was no sea *biscuit*
No furlong for a triple crown

No Conquistador under a flag
Of Iberian royals wanting Indian gold

But untroubled afternoon sun
Happy moments of play
And now and then a biscuit for dogs
Brought over land—not

                        over sea.

MUNICH QUARTET

A group nor famous nor infamous

Only students who play
Some Mozart, some Beethoven—themes
And parts of larger works

One can toss a mark or maybe two
A euro to affirm
Himself/herself a consumer glad
Of harmonious old ideas

Across the *Straße*

We sat and had our *Spaten*

CHAUSSER MAUDIT

Sunday morning

                    church bells sound

And call good Christian worshipers
To *Gottesdienst* now

                        only one Count

Makes no account of it

                     but all across

Rhenish woods a blare of hunstman's horn—
Defiant blast athwart Latin chants—
Sounds a signal call

                     and from deep Hell

Demon hunters hunt the huntsman down

Pursue him to an everlasting panic

Pursue

              panic

A PAUSE AT GARMISCH

Garmisch one summer afternoon
A small round table an umbrella
A sidewalk
Outside a shop

                ice cream for two

Modest fare no doubt but
Alpine relaxation

              and a thought

How could culture go farther?

Now I am sorry I did not
Buy that volume of *Familiennamen*

PROLIFIC

Haydn Mozart Beethoven—not
To mention Bach—how could men compose
So bloody much

                  now you or I

Could use all our days as copyists

Yet

Not copy all one wrote

                      with

                          a goose quill

COCONUT BOYS

After a summer thunderstorm I saw them
On Walton Boulevard and other by-ways
Old West Palm Beach

                            black men, straw hats

A truck, and a small growing load
Of coconuts tossed in as they walked
Slowly behind the truck

                          coconuts

Dropped by a passing storm

A harvest for poor folk

ANTIQUING

Essex on Rte. 133 rain
One welcomed me to browse
Nor so, but open
To any who walk in

              shops

Almost careless of a customer
So many wander in and out

                 so few

Purchase old books records knick-knacks
A lot of canvasses such astronomical
Tags on mundane work

Essex by the Sea some restaurants
Seafood mostly

           a small road

STONE AND THOMAS

Downtown at your flagship store
You made Christmas magic

                    world of toys

American Flyer trains I loved
Because they ran two rails
Not three as Lionel successful rival

                 Every Christmas

Mother took me to your upper floors

Crystal radio sets

Buck Rogers blasters

                 Robbie the Robot
Who spoke by a small crank at the back
"I am Robbie Robot, mechanical man.
Drive me and steer me wherever you can."

All Christmas magic gone

As you are gone

                 now office space

AMBERJACK

Amberjack predator
Game fish and worthy opponent
Mom hooked you
Off Boynton

                an inlet

Open to all fishers

                She pulled

Harder as you opposed
And suddenly
Stopped altogether

                She brought aboard

What was left —

Caput kaput, guts hanging

                A shark

Tore away

Your powerful body

EIN POKAL

A Munich open air café
A young man from Yale
Grandfather's Fatherland

Mir lacht das Abenteuer

A *Pokal* of Mosel

                       pure blonde wine

Cool June evening

PORTLAND CAFÉ

Old classmate, modest lunch
Open air in June

        showy flowers

                our spot

Shade and cool breezes

           Girls

Flaunt summer attire
Walk dogs, chat, look around
Talk with a hand held device

Young women

        so naïve

About their messages

           or not

PORTLAND CAFÉ REDUX

As in München almost
Open air café chat
Wagner Bruckner Strauss

                          Birgit Nilsson

Dance of the Seven Veils

                    her large frame

So agile

                    today not many

Know her, care

And one can have beer at lunch
And that is good
And a breeze can tousle one's hair

And that is

          good

UNCA $CROOGE'S MONEY BIN

Scrooge McDuck *nonpareil* in Duckburg

                              or anywhere

For money

                      oil wells mines
Railroads banks fisheries

A money bin,
Cube atop a hill
A dollar sign
Large on the front

One who owned it
Would be a lucky duck

                    How often

Beagle Boys sweated bullets

Vanitas vanitatum

EXSPECTANS

A boy in Florida our library
Modest stucco structure among palms
A sort of home

Teen hours

        always

                on immaculate sands

Waves caressed our shore

Cumulous towers under a full moon

Puffy

        grand nocturnal glory

                      Florida back then

A love affair

A SUNSET

South of Boynton Inlet
June balmy day
I donned a Squalé mask
In shallow water saw

A conch on the sandy floor

Crawled along the bottom

                              unaware

Of one above him

I swam down, took him

Unable to escape he shrank
Into a cavern,
Hoped I would depart

And so exposed for me
A luminous interior—
Glory of faint mauve and shaded pink

As though a man could watch a sun set
Among pale clouds

                              evening color

Cradled in his palm

INTERLOPER

Spring afternoon, Palm Beach
I donned my Dacor tank
Spat in my Squalé to hold
Fog at bay

        I swam

Among old stumps

           once a pier

A boy at Lido Pools
Swimming lessons — I hardly thought
I would scuba dive, a man,
Across the way among ruins
Of a popular pier

A shadowy form

Out of green haze

A barracuda four feet long and stout

Saw me

YOUR FOURTH

Your Third and **Frei aber Froh**

                                        But now

How slow, how magisterial the andante

Mature wisdom now

                              as though by notes

One could say a final

                              Ja

BEETHOVEN'S BIRTHDAY

Cross Keys High, junior

                             Atlanta

Beethoven's birthday

                             chilly

A record sale

Bought what I could
Septet, Triple Concerto, tucked
Under my arm and once outside
Mother drove me home.

Farewell to Florida miserable I

Adolescent sorrow

ART ἐπ' ἐσχάτου τῶν ἡμερῶν τούτων

Doubt not a moment whatever glory
An American

                may speak of glory

Beyond our native flotsam and jetsam
Trash thrown astern
Refuse of poor taste or
As someone said

                  majoritarian heresy

Glory is *our province* who know

Glory and

            dare be *provincial*

LAKE WORTH AFTER LATIN CLASS

With Roman thoughts

                  to ennoble my soul

Boundless splendor of quotidian skies
Pure undaunted music of palm trees,
Numerous starry nights that offered me
Astonished hours of astronomy,
And Florida's ocean at my beck and call
So I could plunge into her tropic waters
As often as I wanted—and I did—
How could I be unhappy in those days?
There was enough in Florida to calm
And settle me into a peaceful mode.

SOUTHERN COMFORT

A young man I arced over concrete
Above water north of Jacksonville
Trout River

               and saw

A small house among palms

               secluded

On the southern shore
One story, stucco, ochre Spanish tiles
Casa grown old
Among coconut palms

               small palmettos

An archetypal Florida home

Uncumbered days

Watch a Trout flow toward the sea

Harvest a

               windfall coconut

YOU WAIT

Palm Beach Inlet long ago I walked
You waited for me

                  Alone now I wonder
By a bay window as afternoon sun
Warms our living room

A sunny winter day and he is gone

After all assurances have come
And so I have no doubt

                    I know

One I loved has gone to be with you
And so I love him still

Long ago I walked on sand

You saw the wavelets cover my steps

Aware always
Your son with you and our son at your side
A brother

WRIT IN WATER

"Here lies one whose name is writ in water."
—J. KEATS

A famous line—how could it be so wrong?

Famous because wrong

                              no doubt

Ironic invitation to let go
See oneself

                    aright

                         speculum

SEA GRAPE WINE

Could I have a glass

Quaff a mug of sea grape wine and be
A buccaneer of sorts

                    who gathers

Baubles from an ocean bottom
Scotch bonnets mottled cowries, one large conch
Uncommon treasure for a common man

Afterward carouse ashore

Sunset and warm breezes

                at my back

PALM BEACH INTRACOASTAL

Pleasure boats and million dollar yachts
Bound to wooden docks by mooring cables
So they could be available at whim
To those who had the money to afford them

I saw them with a remote sense of longing.
How could I wear a pair of white ducks
And walk across those varnished wooden decks
And hold a stainless steel guard rail
And ride the surge and chaos of the waves
And feel the salty spray upon my face
And be a man who harbored Paradise
In his own soul as he drove out to sea
And challenged all the ocean brought to him?

I was not one to challenge wind or wave.

FRAGMENTS

Fragmentary you are
Nor one out of many

Many out of many

A balance of powers
Your balancing act took, once had

                            character

Your wealth of nations
May obscure

               it has gone missing

Your majority

                 undermines you

Flotsam and jetsam of your coasts
Emblematic

Oceans

        who wash them ashore

More whole than you

PENELOPE BARKER HOUSE

Your history unknown to me

                                        we

Sat on green rockers on your porch
Looked on Edenton Bay and saw
Dead trees in shallow water

                              small boats

Warm sunshine and not a cloud

I read Wordsworth you read

                              what was it

No matter, sun and calm water

Comfort on a morning veranda

Tourists come and go

We slow down

                        savor

MUSIC

"Music has charms to sooth a savage beast."
—CONGREVE, *THE MOURNING BRIDE*,
ACT I, SCENE 1.

Stoppage—I could not put a word
In play to start a poem

        so I thought

Music may do some good—depress a button
And on the radio a violin
And orchestra gush Mendelssohn's concerto

And gush is not a bad word

Romantic

        but good structure

A water wheel and sluice—

A fluent soul

        under control

BOAT IN THE SAND

Prosperity Farms Road
You and I late afternoon

                 ambled

A boat almost a wreck, half sunk
In a large sand lot,
Wonder of sunken architecture
Sunk in sand—you recall

                         Uncle $crooge

And a *Lost Ship of the Desert*
Galleon born on the Colorado
Full of doubloons?

                 or mythical

A fantasy of Conquistadores
Come to plunder Montezuma

                     A boat

Now in a man made lake

Soon to be a marina

PATIO AT NORTH PALM BEACH

Two floors of shops by a marina

Small patio not far from home

Along an open hallway I
Walked above the patio and saw
Angular architecture white and pure
Almost like pictures one had seen of Greece
Of Santorini classically Thera
Of Oia overlooking the Aegean
A place where one could know a holy stillness
A peace apart from other folks
Or so it seemed

        So it was for me

Late that morning as alone
I absorbed sunlight

          on an upturned face

Above a patio.

CUMQUAT BASKET

Small globose suns peep forth
From a forest of green leaves
Southern sunshine for a northern boy

Christmas in Ohio

I could not know one day
Our home would be in Palm Springs
A cumquat tree in our back yard
A grapefruit tree in our front yard

My soul grown subtropical

And sunny as a cumquat

PORTALS

Midnight in Key West — stars so grand
None would believe unless he saw
Large luminaries not dots
As stars show up north

                    Under such heaven

One could observe portals to beyond.
One poet did. But no imagination
Conjures the supernal. That must come
Does come upon us at appointed hours
When you and I on mountain or plateau
A beach, at home or in a hospital
Pass on

            A portal opens and a power

Enfolds

                transports

Whatever *lumina*

                        over Sugarloaf

Or pin points

                    over Cape Ann

SUMMER STORM

Gray clouds tattered in the wind
Zeus or Ba'al Zaphon once rode
And hurled thunderbolts at will

en route

To a holy abode

a mountain palace

On clouds far above hovels
Villages or marble halls

Tattered gods torn and blown away

By One who mounted his chariot and rode
On clouds to help David

as he fled from Saul

And now O storm

you blow my way

SHALLOW SOUL

Soul like an ocean I can only know
As I wade the shallows

                        and look down

And see sand and shell fragments

Waltz around as wavelets play

So I know my soul
Shallow by the shore

Ocean, always father to the waves,
Commote the shallows,

Stir the fragments I embrace

Produce a wavy symphony

More eloquent than I

O VOLUMES

O books O volumes

        almost but not

O tempora O mores and software
Underlines tempora unaware
Of Cicero whose oratory sank
Hapless Cataline

        and Cicero

Could not have foreseen our day

But Cicero in high school was to me
A challenge and a level headed man
And O how simple then a book

        and chalkboard

And Latin students who learned

SENATVS POPVLVSQVE ROMANVS

OUR SHATTERED AGE

No Roman Senate now
Our shattered age and icons all around
Exalted, unimportant or forgotten

Our latest rap, Beethoven or Satchmo

And if many colored shells lay
Or shell fragments all rounded by the sea
Under a subtropical sun for you
Or me or anyone who came along—
Shallow water lapping as we walk—

I would gladly endure the chaos,
Chaos of shell fragments on the shore

An order after all

Formed by sun and sand and sea

Ordering our walk

                        on a warm day

CATHEDRAL OR NAUTILUS

A sonnet can be an oratory
Or any short poem after an epic
An epic a cathedral as it were
Or foundation of one—or a nave
And smaller poems oratories
Sacred spaces not as large

Or better yet, a chambered nautilus,
Submarine shell and a short poem a chamber
And poems added, and the shell grows

No metaphor exactly works

Still

Buoyant shell on accustomed waves
Can offer beauty
To a voyager

EN FUEGO

A small cantina at Del Mar
And we have supper on the patio
December 26

          Above our table
A propane unit radiates warmth
Over us as we share chips and salsa

On undulating turf atop a cliff
Above the sea we saw the sun go down
A turquoise sky and not a cloud
And afterward ambled to our cantina
And our reserved place

              Wood and stucco

Colorful tiles glaze all tables

Mexican ambiance for us who know

No Spanish

ADMIRATION

Some talk of Stevens and although
He is one they prize, or say they do,
They are but fleas

                    To them I say

Be your own dog

A CUP

Ποίημα τῶν ποιητῶν

A cup of the warm south I would now quaff

Or from a thin-stemmed glass and
Show purpureal deeps of sea grape wine

Warm as it stands in the sun

A portion of the wine dark sea
Homerically waits for me
Who built an epic and would be
Like Strauss a hero only he

Was not a primordial maker

Nor am I

BEAUTIFUL THINGS

Joanna's golden ponytail, so long
Almost a temple of the sun to me

Paw paws hanging on a hillside tree,
Just low enough for a young boy to pluck

Palm Beach across from Lido Pools—salt water
Amazingly pristine around her pier

Sunrise over an ocean flat and calm,
And sands unoccupied, at North Palm Beach

Final movement of the *Jupiter*
Virginia loved after school let out

Youthful memories

arrondissements

Of an older poet's thought

FISH STORIES

At lunch in a hotel Grandma and I
Ordered fish and as a small boy

I wondered at the place and could see
The grey Ohio through the window

And Wheeling streets full of business
Cloudy March noon, and snow around.

A teenager in West Palm Beach and
My uncle from Miami and my folks

A restaurant whose name I have forgot
Early March evening a busy spot

I ordered fish and outside afterward
Night traffic, and a rustle of palm fronds

FREEDOM

From small matters —like theology
From small—dare one say it?

Better on a solitary shore
Alone except for palm trees and a lizard
Or two under some round sea grape leaves
On a warm afternoon to look
Across the sand toward a calm ocean

An hour underwater or maybe
A mask and snorkel not a scuba tank
An hour on the surface and a plunge
Or two toward the bottom and a shell
Or two so full of color and beauty
One could see a sunrise or a sunset
In a gold and pink interior

More freedom in the hollow of a shell
Than where theologians dwell

PREPARATORY

Poetry of fronds in the sun
Palms on a beach and calm sea

A theology that finds God
And is from God

A slim volume on aesthetics
God the source of all

Preludes

NEMO'S FARE

20,000 leagues under the sea
Submarine harvest for adventurers
Who cast off

        and want no other menu

Than what a coral reef may offer—
Octopus or clams or wary fish
Who dart away from a diver's arm
But can be had by spear.

          Nemo alone

Fancies that diet and those few
Who ship with him.

        Other fare he offers

Or charges only those

        who dare go down

With him

CONCH MORNING

Young man out of a Mustang
Scuba mask and snorkel in hand

Soles on soft firm sand
I stood on a beach alone

Ocean was a lake
And I about to slake
A hunger to be wet and underwater

Morning sunbeams angled
By refraction among shallows
Sea bottom undulant shadows dance

Crisscross patches of warm sun

An old conch captured in sunlight
A hole or two after ages
Of submarine hardship
Rough rolls underwater hits

Lay open to my hand

I pluck it up
Sand pours out

PELICAN

On a post off Marathon
A pelican sat

        I motored on

                a small boat

Over sand and marl

Solitary on his perch

Sans souci

        he observed

Almost a lone aristocrat

Who soon

        plunged and filled his gullet

SMALL COWRIES

A rented boat off Islamorada
You and I
Rode out — a mild Atlantic
A hot June day
A cumulus tower or two

An old hand I
Scubapro tank firmly on
Squalé mask also

Soon below, a coral canyon
Sandy smooth bottom
And two small cowries
Half lost in sand

Oceanic gems
Splendorous
In the sun
For you

A NEW DAY

A new or another day
A large work done
A small poem now
Opens another door.

Florida Keys an I
A summer afternoon
On a boat could watch
A young sea turtle

Paddle languidly
O to be, and be
In water warm
Cloudy green

WEARY

A last keystroke
A final proof
And has the song
Also gone?

A rustle of palms
A mild ocean breeze
A call of ocean
Florida song

As you summon
Sand and sea
I bow down
Your acolyte

ONCE PARADISE

Summer afternoon
Close cumulus towers
Turquoise sea
A sort of home

And soon
Under two fathoms
Slowly a form
Out of green haze

A large barracuda
Meanders close
Passes and then
A sandy shore

Palm Beach
Long ago
A memory
Or two

ORCHESTRAL COLOR

Russian Easter Overture
Elgar's *In the South*
Till Eulenspiegel and
Pohjola's Daughter

Leonore Number Three
Mother of all
Orchestral color
Tone poems

Tonkunst
Overture
Draw our souls
Elsewhere

MOON AND WAVES

Florida and full moon
Palm Beach water
Popular shore empty
A cone of moon

Across calm seas
Small waves sound
On the sand only
One devoted soul

Stands to watch
As though a goddess
Arose from the sea
As though a man

Could adore her
And be known.
Small waves but waves
Nathless

Sound for her
Sound because
Of her, sound
For me.

HEINRICH'S

Sarasota young mall
Urban world bound to grow
But for now

pax germana

And *Gemütlichkeit*
Heinrich's German Grille
No *Schnellimbiss*
A proper restaurant
Speiseplatz narrow and deep

And deep for thought
And *Politik*
And deeply good

Heinrich der Grosse
Prop.

In whose company
Who chats with our table
One enjoys yet more

Eissbein

and Spaten Lager

SEA GRAPE

Would you be a sea grape
Above Palm Beach
A sunny day
A boardwalk close at hand
American chameleon
Slender green tail
Small alert face
Under your leaf?

SEA OAT

Would you be a sea oat
Above Lake Worth
A sunny day
A sandy path
A brown pelican
Beach guard
Large empty gullet
Close by?

ISLAND SHEAF

O island sheaf or so a poet once
Thought his song or songs.

                              But come to me

Song of some pure island in the Keys
Song of what passes almost immortal

Of sea oats on a shore and no footprints
A solitary place for you, for me

And afterward a table set for two
A table of rattan also sea worn
A sheaf of sea oats, cluster of sea grapes

www.ingramcontent.com/pod-product-compliance
Lightning Source LLC
Chambersburg PA
CBHW071058090426
42737CB00013B/2377